Time Out
for
Holiness
at Home

Other Time Out for Women books by Julie Baker
Time Out for Holiness at Work
Time Out for Prayer
A Pebble in the Pond (available spring, 2001)

Time Out

for

Holiness

at Home

Julie Baker

Cook Communications

Faithful Woman is an imprint of
Cook Communications Ministries, Colorado Springs, Colorado 80918
Cook Communications, Paris, Ontario
Kingsway Communications, Eastbourne, England

TIME OUT FOR HOLINESS AT HOME

Printed in the United States of America.

1 2 3 4 5 6 7 8 9 10 Printing/Year 04 03 02 01 00

Editor: Glenda Schlahta
Cover Design: Jeff Lane
Interior Design: Jeff Lane

ISBN: 0-78143-461-0

Contents

Before You Begin

This book contains ten lessons designed for group study and discussion. It is intended to be facilitated, rather than taught, so the leader doesn't need teaching experience or expertise in the subject matter. The group should plan to meet once a week; advance preparation on the part of the group members is important. Each lesson will take about an hour to complete so that it could be done on a lunch break. The following is a suggested schedule:

ᕁ Welcome and self-introduction of participants

ᕁ Opening prayer
The facilitator may open in prayer or invite someone else to do so, taking care to select someone who is comfortable praying in public.

ᕁ Reflection Questions
These questions are designed to provoke thought rather than promote discussion. However, allow time for members to share brief comments before beginning the study.

ᕁ Introduction
An overview of the passage is provided at the beginning of each lesson to help guide the thinking and discussion of the group through the study time.

ᕁ Study
This section acquaints the group with Bible passages about the topic. The majority of your time should be spent in the **Study** and **Application**.

ᕁ Application
This is an opportunity for participants to choose a course of action that will help them implement what they have learned. The facilitator might set the tone by sharing how she plans to implement what she has learned.

ᕁ Conclusion and Closing Prayer
The facilitator might summarize the lesson in her own words, transitioning into prayer time. Group members can share praise and prayer requests and then spend time praying for each other.

Tips for Group Members

The success of your study group depends on you. These suggestions will help make your time together more enjoyable and more helpful.

➥ Smile. You'll find it mirrored back.

➥ Touching makes people feel significant. Shake hands, pat arms, or give hugs to help others feel valued.

➥ Make eye contact often. It not only connotes honesty and trustworthiness, but also makes people feel significant.

➥ Come prepared. Study the lesson in advance, jot down answers to questions, concerns you have about your job, prayer requests.

➥ Honor each other's comments. Everyone's contribution is valuable. Remember that what is said in the group stays in that room.

➥ Participate in the discussion and stick to the subject. If you tend to dominate conversations, excercise self-control and practice listening to what others have to say. If you're quiet, make an effort to join in the discussion.

➥ During prayer time, share your praise and requests. You might want to jot down the prayer requests of others and pray for them during the week.

Tips for Facilitators

People learn best where they feel comfortable and welcome and where their needs are being considered. Keeping the following in mind will help you provide that atmosphere.

⤚ Smile. You'll find it mirrored back.

⤚ Touching makes people feel significant. Shake hands, pat arms, or give hugs to help participants feel welcome and valued.

⤚ Make eye contact often. It not only connotes honesty and trustworthiness, but also makes people feel significant.

⤚ Did you know it takes eleven positive comments to erase one criticism? Your compliment may be the only kind word your participants hear that day! Have a policy in the group that no one is put down for her contributions. Make your study group a safe, inviting place for women to talk about their concerns.

⤚ Establish a policy of confidentiality. What is said in the group stays in that room.

⤚ Encourage everyone to participate in discussion. Use open-ended questions: Why do you think that? What do you mean by . . . ? Give an example. Draw the quieter women into discussion, and help those who dominate the discussion to exercise control.

⤚ During prayer time, encourage each woman to offer one praise; then allow the needs of the group to surface. Group members might want to jot down the prayer requests so that they can pray for them during the week.

⤚ Ask the Holy Spirit to give you discernment regarding the needs in the group. A midweek phone call for progress on a prayer request goes a long way toward making people feel cared for.

⌐ The room arrangement can make people feel either included or lectured to. Arrange seating in such a way as to create a feeling of intimacy and inclusion.

⌐ Everyone appreciates organization. Stick to the time limit and come fully prepared.

⌐ Take time during the week to pray specifically for your Bible study group: for individual and group needs, as well as for the overall goal of insight into God's Word.

Introduction

Holiness. It's a word we hear at church, stumble across in the Bible . . . but what does it really mean?

Webster defines *holy* as being "perfect in goodness and righteousness."[1] Well, okay—that's suitable as a description of God. But in Leviticus 11:44, God tells us, "Be holy, because I am holy."

Now, wait a minute! That's impossible, isn't it? W.E. Vine, author of *Vine's Expository Dictionary of Old and New Testament Words*, gives us a definition that is a little easier to live with. He says that holiness "signifies separation to God" and "the conduct befitting those so separated."[2] In other words, it means acting like the children of God that we are!

That still isn't always easy. But fortunately, we have God's grace to catch us when we fall. The day we accept God's forgiveness through Christ, we are counted as holy in His eyes. But the rest of our lives on earth is a journey during which we move closer to the actual daily practice of that holiness and further away from being mired in sinful habits. Sometimes we feel we are beginning to get the hang of it; other days, it seems it will never happen. But the Holy Spirit is with us always, and we know that "he who began a good work in [us] will carry it on to completion" (Phil. 1:6).

Holiness in our lives pleases God . . . but sometimes—when anger boils up inside us, or when temptation's pull seems irresistible—that just isn't enough motivation. It should be, of course. But God knows how weak we are, and He knows how self-oriented we can be. And so His Word helps us see that holiness benefits us directly, as well. It makes our relationships more enjoyable, our finances more stable, our recreation more fun; it even gives us a better shot at having good physical health. And God's Word not only provides motivation; it also provides the how-to, both directly and indirectly, in the form of examples. And those how-tos are what this study guide is all about.

Lord, I thank You for each woman who has made a commitment to be drawn into a holy relationship with you. I pray that You would open her eyes to Your truths and that You would place in her heart the enthusiasm and joy that comes from seeking You. Bless her family, her health, her talents, and her efforts to serve You. Most of all, give her the desire and discipline to be obedient to You.

In Jesus' name, Amen.

Julie Baker

1 *Webster's Ninth New Collegiate Dictionary* (Springfield, Mass.: Merriam-Webster Inc., 1986) 576.
2 W.E. Vine, *Vine's Expository Dictionary of Old and New Testament Words* (Nashville: Royal Publishers, Inc., 1939).

ONE

Developing Personal Holiness

*I*n this study, we'll learn how holiness in our lives can make a difference, and we will look at ways to go about bringing holiness into various areas. Before we get that specific, though, let's take a look at what is meant by the term *holiness*—and see how to bring it into our hearts.

Reflection Question

When you hear the phrase *personal holiness*, what comes to your mind?

God Comes to my mind —
It means to me + trying to do
what would give the world
an idea of what Christ is
+ means in my life
No flirting — no stealing
No lying — No

Introduction

The command to "be holy, because I am holy," in Leviticus 11:44, must have frustrated the dickens out of Old Testament followers of God—either that or made them want to give up before they even started trying. After all, who can possibly be as holy as God? The answer, of course, is no one. So why does He even ask us to try? There are at least two reasons: one is to show us what the standard is; the other is to show us how completely unable we are to attain that standard. When we understand those two things, our need for a Savior is perfectly clear. Unholiness separates us from God; forgiveness through Christ Jesus reunites us. The New Testament doesn't let us off the hook, however. Romans 12:1 tells us to "offer [our] bodies as living sacrifices, holy and pleasing to God." But what does that mean? Is it ever possible? Let's find out.

Study

Read together Colossians 3:1-10; 1 Thessalonians 4:1-12; 1 Peter 1:13-25; and 1 John 5:17-21.

1. Based on these passages, how would you now define *holiness?*

2. First John 1:8 says, "If we claim to be without sin, we deceive ourselves and the truth is not in us." This is not news to most of us! Fortunately, once we accept Christ's atonement for our sins, we are forgiven, not only for the sins we have already committed, but for all the sins we ever will commit (Eph. 1:7, 2:8-9). How can you reconcile this truth, however, with the notion of purification in 1 Peter 1:22 and Philippians 2:12?

≈ What is our role in purification?

3. According to 1 Peter 1:13, is holiness something that will occur naturally once Christ is in our lives? Restate this verse in your own words.

〜 How do you "prepare your minds for action"?

〜 This passage also advises us to be self-controlled. What role do you think self-control plays in holiness?

4. First Peter 1:14 admonishes us not to "conform to the evil desires you had when you lived in ignorance." What are some of the evil desires that lure us?

5. What do you think 1 Peter 1:17 means when it tells us to live our lives here as strangers?

☙ How does that admonishment relate to personal holiness? (See also Rom. 8:5).

6. What does Colossians 3:1-10 tell us to "put to death," or rid ourselves of?

☙ How can the advice in verse 1 help us to do that?

Application

These passages on holiness were written to the early Christians who lived in a culture that was every bit as corrupt as our own. Much of what is written in these passages may seem obvious to you, but it didn't to first-century readers. And it may not to many people today. Even if you know these passages about holiness, it's one thing to have a high moral standard in your mind; it's quite another to have one in your life. Let's take what we've learned and put it into practice.

1. First Thessalonians 4:1-12 offers a number of things we can do to incorporate holiness into our lives. From the list below, choose the three or four instructions you struggle with most. Describe what you think they mean and discuss practical ways to implement them.

☙ Avoid sexual immorality.

← Do not take advantage of your brother or sister.

← Don't be impure.

← Love others.

← Lead a quiet life.

← Mind your own business.

← Work hard.

~ Live in a way that wins respect.

2. One area most of us struggle with is the control of our bodies, yet this is such a fundamental part of our lives, one that influences every other aspect. First Corinthians 6:19-20 says, "Do you not know that your body is a temple of the Holy Spirit, who is in you, whom you have received from God? You are not your own; you were bought at a price. Therefore honor God with your body." How can you honor God in the following physical areas?

Diet. Okay, admit it—you keep Little Debbies in your desk drawer or you visit the vending machine every afternoon or you're more likely to eat five servings of fruit and vegetables in a week than you are in a day . . . right? Maybe you've just grown dependent on caffeine. God has given us amazing bodies, but they won't keep being amazing if we don't take care of them. What one change could you make that would improve your overall nutritional health?

Exercise. Work, kids, dishes, laundry . . . it's hard to fit exercise into the daily mad dash. Apart from the obvious benefits, though, don't you want to give God a strong, healthy temple to inhabit? If you already have an exercise routine you're satisfied with, write down the things that tend to get you off track, as well as a plan for how to get around them. If you don't, choose just one form of exercise to incorporate into your life, something as simple as walking or gardening. Write down when you are going to do it, aiming for at least twenty minutes, three times a week.

Sex. Men aren't the only ones who face temptation in this area. What tends to stir up your passions in ways you aren't proud of—novels, magazines, movies? Sexuality is meant to be a source of great pleasure in our lives, but only in the proper context. How can you make sure you are channeling it in the right direction?

Conversation. An old Chinese proverb says that a man's tongue is only six inches long, but it can kill a man six feet tall. Our tongue may be a small part of our body, but it can sure do a lot of damage! (See Prov. 18:21.) Do you struggle most with gossip, swearing, or sharpness of speech? Maybe you tend to lose your temper and say things you regret, or perhaps you tend to bend the truth. Pinpoint one goal in this area.

Relaxation. It doesn't seem like something we should need reminding of, does it? But so often, relaxation falls to the bottom of our to-do list. Yet it's through rest that we are able to regain control of so many other areas—our stress level, temper, even eating habits. Our bodies weren't meant to go nonstop, so give yours a break! Decide on one thing you could do each day to give yourself a time-out—maybe take a soak bath, lie down with a book or magazine while the spaghetti boils, or take the dog for a solitary stroll around the block—even for ten minutes.

Josh McDowell has said that every command in the Bible is for either our *protection* or our *provision*. All these admonishments for holy living can seem like a burden at first glance. Choose several of the instructions in this lesson and discuss how they could ultimately result in your protection or your provision.

Conclusion

Dr. Robert Schuller coined the phrase, "Inch by inch, everything's a cinch." None of us will achieve personal holiness overnight; it's a lifetime project—one that will not be complete until we are in heaven. But by taking small steps toward improving personal holiness, we are moving in the right direction in the process of sanctification. Move that first inch forward today, won't you?

Memory Verse

"Do you not know that your body is a temple of the Holy Spirit, who is in you, whom you have received from God? You are not your own; you were bought at a price. Therefore honor God with your body" (1 Cor. 6:19-20).

Two

Holiness with My Husband

On our wedding day, standing next to a handsome, tuxedoed man who was slipping a diamond on my finger, the vows I made seemed ridiculously easy, like promising to always brush my teeth or make my bed. Yes, I'd been told that times might get tough—and envisioned a car accident leaving him paralyzed, with me by his bedside stroking his hair, brave and steadfast in my sacrificial devotion.

What I didn't imagine was how day-to-day life would relegate romance to the back burner . . . for months or years at a time. Or how balancing the checkbook could invoke days of stony silence. Or how carpools and workdays and socks on the floor would drain the conversation right out of us, until neither of us remembered what we used to talk about, or why we even wanted to. Those are the hard times married people alluded to. They're the ones most likely to undermine our marriages, and they're the hardest circumstances in which to remain holy. Today, try to remember your vows as you revisit God's design for marriage.

Reflection Questions
What is your idea of a holy wife?

What does it mean to be submissive to your husband?

Introduction

In our discrimination-wary society, the idea of submission seems pretty out of date. Even the traditional view of marriage associated with the Bible is looking passé as our society redefines words like *marriage* and *family*. Yet the Bible is God's timeless truth, relevant to every culture and every generation. So how can we apply the truths of the Bible in the society we live in? First, it's important to recognize that people's interpretations of biblical ideas are not necessarily correct, even if they've been widely held for decades. And second, we need to remember that, as Solomon said, "there is nothing new under the sun" (Eccl. 1:9). Our culture has not thought up anything God hasn't seen before, and the changing face of our society doesn't nullify God's commands.

So let's look at what God says about a wife's role in marriage. And then let's look at two stories of wives in the Bible who handled troubling situations in different ways. Finally, we'll put those things together for principles we can live by when it comes to holiness in relationship to our husbands.

Study

Read together 1 Peter 3:1-9 and Proverbs 31.

1. First Peter 3:3 tells us that a wife's beauty should not come from "outward adornment," but Proverbs 31 says that a "wife of noble character" wears "fine linen and purple." How can you reconcile this apparent contradiction?

᠊᠍ Look through both passages for references to beauty or appearance. Do you think a wife's appearance is important? Explain the reasons for your answer.

᠊᠍ What things contribute to her looks?

2. When we think of someone who is submissive, we often envision a mouselike creature with low self-esteem, few opinions of her own, and utter dependence on the one she submits to. Does this mesh with the description of the woman in Proverbs 31? Write a definition of submission based on this passage.

⌐ In what ways do you think that the Proverbs 31 woman was submissive to her husband? Give reasons for your answer.

3. Proverbs 31:23 seems to stick out like a sore thumb in this passage. How does it apply to this description of a godly wife?

4. First Peter 3:6 urges us not to "give way to fear" when it comes to submission to our husbands. Why might someone fear being submissive? What would you say to a newly married woman who expresses fear about submission?

⌐ Are there times when we ought not to submit? If you answer yes, give examples.

5. In 1 Peter 3:7, what safeguard does God put in place for wives as we submit to our husbands? How does this safeguard protect us? (See also Eph. 5:25.)

⤺ Verse 7 refers to wives as the "weaker partner," a description that has riled many a woman. But, generally speaking, women *are* physically weaker than men—and, in this passage and others, they are given less power than men in the relationship. Keeping these things in mind, discuss why and in what ways you think husbands are asked to take our relative "weakness" into consideration.

⤺ If our husbands do not follow the admonishment in verse 7, are we released from following the instruction to submit? Give *scriptural* reasons for your answer.

6. Now read 1 Samuel 25:2-44 and Acts 4:32–5:11.

⤺ Describe the character of Nabal. *Always looking for a fight & was mean in his dealings forgetful - Did not repay kindness with kindness*

⤺ Describe the character of Abigail. *Smart beautiful*

✐ Describe the character of Ananias.

✐ Describe the character of Sapphira.

✐ Of the two wives, which do you think was more godly?

✐ Which do you think was more submissive?

✐ Which wife do you think God was more pleased with? Why do you think so?

✐ What does this tell you about how and when to apply the 1 Peter passage?

Application

1. According to what we've studied today, where does your first loyalty lie?

❧ Under what circumstances is it *appropriate* to not submit to your husband's wishes?

❧ Under what circumstances would it be *inappropriate* to not submit?

2. Reread 1 Peter 3:8-9. Which of these attributes do you currently struggle with most in your relationship with your husband?

3. Abigail obviously understood that we are responsible before God for our own actions, regardless of the actions of our spouse. How does this truth relate to your own situation?

4. Discuss the following scenarios and brainstorm ways you might handle them in light of what you've learned in this study.

⮑ Your husband is not a Christian, although he is a loving, caring man who generally shows good judgment. He has an opportunity for advancement in his career, but it would mean a move for your family. He wants to take the job, but you don't think you should make any major decision without praying about it first. Should you hold him to what you feel you are hearing from God, or respect his desire in the matter?

⮑ Your husband is a believer, but he is not, in your opinion, living by 1 Peter 3:7. You've tried to point this out to him, but he has been unresponsive, and, in general, you are in a rocky place in your marriage. Are you obligated to live by verses 1-6? Why?

Conclusion

In John 13:34, Christ told us to love one another as He has loved us. That one command, if we really followed it, would make an immeasurable difference in most of our marriages. The sacrifices we make for our husbands sometimes feel huge—two kids instead of three, this house instead of that one, even a faraway state instead of the one where we grew up. But these sacrifices are minute in comparison to the one Christ made for us. He sacrificed His life, and in the most humiliating, torturous way possible. He showed us by example that when we commit ourselves to someone, we treasure him, and we act in his best interest, even when it is at great cost to ourselves—and even when the other person is, like us, imperfect and not always worthy or appreciative of it. No matter how much or how well we love our spouse, our first loyalty lies with Christ . . . but most of the time, the way we show that best is by loving our husband as Christ loves us.

Memory Verse

"Live in harmony with one another; be sympathetic, love as brothers, be compassionate and humble. Do not repay evil with evil or insult with insult, but with blessing, because to this you were called so that you may inherit a blessing"
(1 Peter 3:8-9).

THREE

Holiness with My Children

*Y*ou felt you'd never known what love was when they placed that tiny, helpless bundle in your arms for the first time. You were outraged at reports of parental abuse. You smiled at a future full of sunshine and childish laughter. Until the day your baby screamed for three hours straight. And in the back of your mind, you felt the tiniest hint of understanding for the woman who went to the movies and left her baby home alone. And then when your second child came along and that idyllic sibling relationship disintegrated into punches and name calling, you knew you were completely inadequate for the job of parenting—your only hope was that no one would notice. Gone were the dreams of well-mannered children who loved God and each other and did well in school. You were just hoping to keep them alive and out of prison! In this study, we'll try to recapture those feelings of love and a bright future, and we'll see how holiness can help bring those dreams into reality.

Reflection Questions

What are the greatest challenges you face as a parent?

What are the qualities of holiness that you want to see instilled in your children?

In what areas of your relationship with your children would you like to see improvement?

Introduction

Children are important to God. Look in your concordance at the number of biblical references to children and childbearing; the entire book of Proverbs is a letter from a father to his son. Numerous passages throughout the Bible are directed to parents about their children and to children about their parents. So why do we so often want to throw up our hands in despair when it comes to parenting? Perhaps because we get so caught up in the crisis of the moment that we forget that God is with us, waiting for us to ask His advice, wanting to give us His help.

This lesson is about finding that help—and about gaining God's holy perspective on both our children and our parenting problems.

Study

1. When we struggle with parenting issues, the first place to look for solutions is the Bible. Many of the verses are as familiar as our own children's faces, but they bear looking at again and again. Study each of the following passages. What is the main message in each one?

~ Exodus 34:7

~ Deuteronomy 6:4-9

∾ Psalm 78:1-8

∾ Proverbs 22:15

∾ Proverbs 29:15

∾ Matthew 18:6-7

∾ Ephesians 6:4

∾ Colossians 3:21

⤚ 1 Timothy 5:8

⤚ 2 Timothy 3:15

2. After reading these passages, how would you define *holiness* as it relates to parenting?

Application
1. Look again at the verses above. Select the ones you currently need to apply the most.

⤚ How could you implement the instructions in those verses?

2. We often put away for safekeeping the treasures of our children's early years. Their special blankies are folded on a shelf with a favorite teddy nestled in beside them; their first attempts at drawing and writing are tucked away in boxes, all in readiness to hand over at some milestone of growing up. And we save favorite possessions of our own, planning to someday pass them down as well, hoping that our children will value them as we have. These material heirlooms are priceless, but perhaps even more meaningful are the ones that exist only in our hearts and minds—the confident courage of a grandmother, the steadfast patience of an aunt, your mother's unwavering commitment to what was right. . . .

⤚ What "heirlooms" stand out in your mind as you reflect on your family of origin? If applicable, list the negative ones as well as the positive.

⤚ What "heirlooms" are your children collecting under your care? (Read Ps. 78:1-8 again.)

⤚ What "heirlooms" would you like for them to accumulate?

3. Deuteronomy 6:4-9 tells us to teach our children about God as we "sit at home" and as we "walk along the road." You probably spend a good deal of time "walking (or driving) along the road," but if you're like most parents, you're more likely to be refereeing arguments than teaching godly truths. How could you make this a more positive, productive time?

❧ In this age of soccer games, piano lessons, and ballet classes filling every extracurricular moment, it's difficult to find time just to "sit at home." Evaluate your schedule. Does it allow time for being together in your own home, doing nothing planned or organized? It's in those "sitting around" moments that some of the most significant conversations happen. If you are too busy for those moments to happen, what could you eliminate? change?

4. The Deuteronomy passage also tells us to teach our kids as we lie down at night and as we get up in the morning. What is your family's morning routine like? What could you do to help it go more smoothly?

❧ What could you incorporate into the morning routine that would be a reminder for your children to include God in their day? (For example: sitting down to breakfast together and asking a blessing; playing Christian music that your kids like on the stereo; reading a brief daily devotional together.)

∼ What is your nighttime routine like? How could you help it go more smoothly?

∼ How could you help your children end their day with God in their minds? (For instance: praying with them; providing Christian music or story tapes to listen to as they fall asleep; leaving a nightly note on their pillows with an encouraging Bible verse on it.)

5. God, our Heavenly Father, says for us to be holy because He is holy (Lev. 11:44). There's a lesson in that statement for us as earthly parents. If we want our children to live holy lives, we need to live holy lives as well. Are there areas of unholiness in your life that are setting an example you'd rather your children not follow?

6. What is currently your most difficult issue with regard to parenting? Ask your group to pray for you.

Conclusion

Developing holiness in our children begins with developing holiness in ourselves. Children model what they see. When they face troubled waters in their own lives, they will remember vividly how we handled those times. When they are faced with choices, they will instinctively know what we would choose. When they are setting priorities, they will know from experience where our priorities lie. None of us is perfect. But we are all capable of presenting an overall picture of what we really value in life . . . and if it's holiness, our children's inheritance will be a rich one indeed.

Memory Verse

"Hear, O Israel: The Lord our God, the Lord is one. Love the Lord your God with all your heart and with all your soul and with all your strength. These commandments that I give you today are to be upon your hearts. Impress them on your children. Talk about them when you sit at home and when you walk along the road, when you lie down and when you get up. Tie them as symbols on your hands and bind them on your foreheads. Write them on the doorframes of your houses and on your gates" (Deut. 6:4-9).

Four

Holiness with My Neighbors

There was a time, not too far in our country's past, when neighborhoods were communities. Extended family lived down the block, everyone's dogs roamed the sidewalks, and all the houses had front porches. Backyards didn't have fences, and nobody needed a Block Parent sign in the window. Everyone looked out for everyone anyway.

Well, maybe it wasn't quite that idyllic. But fences and cars and frequent moves have changed a lot about the way our neighborhoods feel. We all have our own separate lives, and we don't really need our neighbors anymore. Or do we? It's easy to look at people coming and going and think their lives are really as "together" as they appear, but unless we get to know them, we have no idea what really lies behind the curtains or the closed garage door. As Christians, we have what people need. But unless we get acquainted, we'll never have the chance to give it to them.

Reflection Questions

How would you characterize your relationship with your neighbors:

close and familiar

friendly from a distance

nonexistent

How do you think your neighbors perceive you?

Introduction

The Bible gives us guidelines for all kinds of relationships, including the ones with our neighbors. It also gives us goals. Let's dig into the Scriptures for ways to develop holy relationships with those who live near us. And let's seek inspiration to, as Paul says, "shine like stars in the universe as [we] hold out the word of life" (Phil. 2:15).

Study

Read Leviticus 19:15-18; Luke 10:25-37; and 2 Peter 1:5-10.

1. How do you think we are to define the word *neighbor?*

2. From these passages, what attitudes do you think would be present in a good neighbor?

⌐ What kinds of actions are expected of a good neighbor?

⌐ Why do you think each of these items was included?

3. What attitudes or actions are we warned against in these passages?

⮑ Look at these one by one. Why do you think they were included?

4. The Leviticus passage gives us permission to voice our concerns with our neighbor, but that doesn't mean shouting matches across the hedge are acceptable. Describe the manner and attitudes with which we should address problems.

⮑ Is there any indication what kinds of problems should be addressed? What other passages are related to the issue of confrontation? Use your concordance.

5. The 2 Peter passage doesn't specifically talk about neighbors. How does developing these qualities in your life make you a better neighbor?

6. Do you think we are required to become close friends with our neighbors? Describe the kind of relationship you think God wants us to have with our neighbors.

7. How will our neighbors benefit if we follow the instructions in these passages?

⌒ How will we benefit?

Application

1. The Good Samaritan did not live or work near the injured traveler, yet Jesus identified the men as neighbors. It's doubtful that the Good Samaritan was just out for an afternoon stroll that day; he apparently had business to attend to, since he arranged for the man's care until he could return. Yet he took the time to attend to the situation.

Sometimes we are so busy or preoccupied that we simply can't get off the treadmill long enough to stop and help someone in need—if we even have the presence of mind to realize the need exists. Do you have enough leeway in your life to allow for unanticipated needs? If not, what could you do to free up some time and energy so that you can be available for the unexpected?

2. Whom would you identify as being your neighbors on a consistent basis?

3. In what ways are you exemplifying the neighborly attitudes and actions we've studied to these people?

4. Are there any areas in which your neighborliness needs work? What could you do to be more neighborly?

5. Your neighborhood, in the spiritual sense, may be the block you live on, your child's school, your workplace, even your exercise class. It may be all of the above, or any number of other places. For this exercise, though, choose just one. What could you do to promote a feeling of community among these people?

6. Discuss the following scenarios in light of this study.

⤳ The neighbors next door let their dog roam the neighborhood. Unfortunately, it has come to view your front yard as its restroom. What should you say or do?

⤳ A couple has moved in across the street—a couple of men. It is evident that they are homosexual. How should you handle it?

⤳ A family down the block has middle-school-aged children who come home to an empty house after school. In the hours before their parents come home, you've noticed the kids outside smoking, and their house also seems to be the teen hang-out. You're concerned about the lack of supervision. Is this any of your business?

Conclusion

We can't meet the needs of everyone around us. Some days we just can't drop what we're doing, no matter what the need or who has it. And we can't feel solely responsible for making sure everyone around us hears about Christ. But in general, if we scale back our lives so that our schedules have some flexibility, if we open our eyes to the peripheral view instead of focusing so intently on our own objectives, if we look for ways to show compassion and mercy . . . we'll be the kind of neighbors God wants us to be. And who can predict the blessings that will bring?

Memory Verse

"Do not seek revenge or bear a grudge against one of your people, but love your neighbor as yourself" (Lev. 19:18).

FIVE

Holiness with My Relatives

*R*elating with relatives can bring great pleasure . . . but it can also bring frustration. With your own extended family, just being in their presence can bring to the surface all the mixture of feelings you had in childhood. With your husband's extended family, there's the tricky balance of being family, yet not quite. Sometimes we'd just like to leave the whole mess behind. But whether your family feels like a blessing or a curse, you belong to them, and they to you. And there are certain guidelines to follow in dealing with them. Let's see what they are.

Reflection Questions

How would you describe your relationship with your extended family?

Do your relatives share your religious views and value system?

Are there relationships that are strained or difficult to maintain?

What changes would you like to see within the relationships between you and your relatives?

Introduction

If you go to an exhaustive concordance of the Bible and look up *relative, father, mother,* and *family*, you will find more references than you could study in one sitting, or even several. The Lord clearly has much to say on the subject! Some of His advice is given to us in pictures, through stories. Some of it is stated directly, in the form of commands. Some of it deals with family members who are easy to love and some of it deals with those who are not. But regardless of their behavior—whether they are godly or ungodly, good relatives or bad—there are some over-riding principles for how we are to treat them.

Study

Read Exodus 18:24, 20:12; Leviticus 19:32; Ruth 1:1-19; Proverbs 17:6, 23:22; Mark 3:31-35; Ephesians 5:31; 1 Timothy 5:3-4, 16; James 2:14-17.

1. According to these passages, who qualifies as family?

↪ Is there a one-size-fits-all definition of family? Explain your answer based on the Scriptures you read about family.

2. From what you've just read, do your priorities lie with your extended family or with your immediate family (your husband and children)?

3. What is our obligation toward our relatives?

4. What do you think is meant by the term *honor*?

~ Do you think there is any difference between the terms *honor*, *respect*, and *obey*? If so, explain these differences.

5. What kind of help are we asked to give our family members? Who in particular should we assist?

Application
1. Do you have any relatives who currently live on an extremely limited income? Based on what you've read today, what is your obligation to them?

2. Do you have any relatives who are emotionally bereft right now, or who may be lonely? If so, what is your obligation to them?

3. We are told to honor our older relatives. Do you think there should be any difference in the way we carry out this command if they are godly versus ungodly?

4. Perhaps, like Ruth and Naomi, relations who have been important to you—perhaps a parent or husband or sibling—have died. How did Ruth and Naomi help each other fill the emptiness left from the death of their husbands and Naomi's son? Has He put others into your life who have helped fill the void? If so, list them here. If not, look more closely—there may be someone you haven't noticed! If you still can't think of anyone, ask God to provide that person for you.

5. While maintaining relationships with our extended families is important, the Scriptures are also quite clear that we are to make our immediate family our priority. Is this difficult for you? In what ways? Are there ways in which you need to "leave and cleave" (Gen. 2:24)? Be specific.

6. Evaluate the following scenarios in light of what we have studied.

‹ Your in-laws are well-meaning, godly people, but they are constantly offering you and your husband advice regarding your personal affairs. You find this intrusive, although you have to admit their advice is generally good. What should you do?

‹ Your parents are alcoholics. Throughout their lives, they have made poor choices, especially financially. They are now beyond working age, and their retirement income is very limited. Should you supplement it? If so, to what degree?

‹ Your brother-in-law has been in and out of drug rehab programs several times over the years, and he has just completed another one. He has no job and no place to live. Should you take him into your home? If so, under what conditions?

‹ Your elderly aunt, whom you dearly love, is unable to live alone any longer. She requires assistance with almost every element of her care. You hate to see her go into a nursing home, but you have young children at home. What should you do?

꙳ Your parents are having a fiftieth wedding anniversary celebration. The week before, your teen-age daughter's soccer team wins a local championship, and the regional play-offs will be the same day as the party. Due to location, it would be impossible to attend both. What do you choose? What will you require your daughter to do?

Memory Verse

"Rise in the presence of the aged, show respect for the elderly and revere your God. I am the Lord" (Lev. 19:32).

SIX

Holiness with My Finances

With the abundance of goods and gadgets and credit cards available to us today—and especially with the pervasiveness of advertising—the temptation to spend hits us from every side, no matter where we go. You might think we're the first generation to be consumed with money issues, but money has presented problems since the beginning of time. It's been said that two-thirds of Jesus' teachings in the Bible concerned money matters, and that doesn't even include what the Old Testament and the Epistles have to say. So let's take a look at what the Bible says about money and see what we can learn.

Reflection Questions

How would you describe financial holiness?

What aspect of money management is most difficult for you? What makes it difficult?

Introduction

Greed, generosity, security . . . if it pertains to money, it's in the Bible. We can't possibly look at every verse that mentions money in this brief space, but we can study enough to give us an idea of how God wants us to handle our finances, and how we can do it with holiness.

Study

Read Deuteronomy 14:22-29; Malachi 3:8-12; Matthew 25:14-30; Luke 21:1-4; 2 Corinthians 9:6-15; 1 Timothy 6:9-10.

1. From what you've just read, describe the attitude you think God wants us to have toward money.

2. Describe the attitude we are to have about giving.

3. What do you think is meant by the phrase "love of money" (1 Tim. 6:10)?

4. What results from the pursuit of riches?

5. What results from generosity and tithing?

⮑ What is our tithe to be used for?

⮑ What is the reason for tithing?

⮑ Does tithing pertain only to money? Explain your answer.

6. Describe the attitude we are to have about giving.

Application

1. Do you think tithing is required of modern-day Christians? Why or why not?

↷ What aspect of tithing (or giving generously) is most difficult for you?

2. Have you ever thought about tithing in ways other than financially—for instance, with your time or your abilities? Give examples of how you might do that.

3. Tithing reminds us to revere God and put Him first. When we choose not to give, it can be an indication that what we are not willing to give up is more important to us than He is. Is there anything you currently are placing above the Lord in importance?

4. Sometimes we make financial decisions that preclude our being able to give generously or tithe: for example, buying a car or a house that takes too big a chunk out of our monthly paycheck. Is there anything in your budget that is pulling the belt a little too snug? What could you change so that your priorities can fall back into place?

5. If there has been a time when you have made your "giving" check the first one you wrote each month, what do you recall about that period of your life?

~ If you have discontinued the practice, what caused you to stop?

Conclusion

The Bible seems to be filled with contradictions: if we die, we live; by losing, we gain; when we give, we receive. Ecclesiastes 11:1 says to cast your bread upon the water and it will return to you. Proverbs 22:9 states that "a generous man will himself be blessed, for he shares his food with the poor." Have you ever noticed that you simply cannot out-give God? The only way to stop the flood of God's blessings is to stop doing what He asks. Logic tells us to hang on to what we have, but if we do, that's all we'll end up with. When we give, we receive more than we had to begin with—maybe not in the same form, but certainly in greater quantity. Givers may or may not have full pockets . . . but their hearts are never empty.

Memory Verse

From the list below, choose the verse that speaks most to you at the present time.

"Honor the Lord with your wealth, with the firstfruits of all your crops; then your barns will be filled to overflowing, and your vats will brim over with new wine" (Prov. 3:9-10).

"Do not withhold good from those who deserve it, when it is in your power to act. Do not say to your neighbor, 'Come back later; I'll give it tomorrow'— when you now have it with you" (Prov. 3:27-28).

"Better a little with the fear of the Lord than great wealth with turmoil" (Prov. 15:16).

"Humility and the fear of the Lord bring wealth and honor and life" (Prov. 22:4).

"Cast but a glance at riches, and they are gone, for they will surely sprout wings and fly off to the sky like an eagle" (Prov. 23:5).

"He who gives to the poor will lack nothing, but he who closes his eyes to them receives many curses" (Prov. 28:27).

SEVEN

Holiness in My Recreation

*W*ork hard, then play hard! That seems to be the motto of our society, and it really isn't a bad one. But it begs two questions: Do you really ever get to the "play hard" part? And if you do, could your play be considered holy?

Reflection Questions

What is recreation?

How could recreation be considered holy or unholy?

Introduction

The Bible has a lot to say about how we relate, how we worship, how we give, how we work . . . and it also covers how we play. What exactly is recreation? Webster defines it as "refreshment of strength or spirit after work; *also:* a means of refreshment or diversion."[1] Boy, sounds like just what the doctor ordered, doesn't it? For all the money spent on entertainment in this country, most of us—especially Christians, it seems—aren't really very good at recreating. We might go to a restaurant, but it's with a client, or it's purely for the purpose of a quick meal between activities. There may be an RV in the driveway, but it rarely sees a national park. We take a day off, but we spend it doing errands or painting the house. Hard work is certainly a virtue, but the Scriptures also place a high value on rest. Let's see what they have to say.

Study

Read Exodus 23:12, 31:12-17, 34:21; Leviticus 23:24-25, 39-41; Esther 9:17; Psalm 19:7, 23:3; Hebrews 4:9-11; and Philippians 4:8.

1. There are two kinds of rest: physical rest and spiritual, or emotional, rest. Define each type of rest in light of what you've just read.

➥ Physical rest:

➥ Emotional/spiritual rest:

2. When we think of rest, what often comes to mind is a nap! Or a long, languid afternoon in the hammock with a good book and a tall glass of iced tea. There's nothing wrong with this picture, but what else does the Bible say rest might entail? Besides helping us gear up to go at it again, what is the purpose of rest?

3. Why do you think rest in the Bible is so often associated with feasts and celebrations?

4. The Puritans helped us associate Christianity with long faces and sober attire and demure behavior. Is this the picture you get from the passages you just read? If not, what picture does come into your mind?

5. What do you think it means to be restored? (Ps. 23:3)

🖎 How do you think this happens?

6. What criteria do you think should apply when we are choosing what form of rest to take? See Philippians 4:8.

Application

1. What is your favorite form of recreation?

⏴ Does it meet the criteria for godly relaxation? Why or why not?

2. If you've read much of the Gospels or the Old Testament, you know that the Bible is full of parties. Jewish wedding feasts, in fact, often lasted a week or more. The implication is that God enjoys a good celebration, and He thinks it's healthy for us to have lots of them! No doubt you mark birthdays and anniversaries and holidays with events *called* celebrations—but do you *really* celebrate these things? Or are you just going through the motions?

⇌ What difference might it make if you were to truly focus on *celebrating* rather than on having a party, a dinner out, and so on? What could you do differently to make events feel more like celebrations?

3. While we may not take a day a week for it, most of us do get around to resting our bodies—eventually. But how often do we rest our souls? What do you think it means to rest your soul?

⇌ How might you go about it?

4. Evaluate your present forms of recreation. Do they restore your body? If not, what could you do to make sure your body is getting the rest it needs?

⇌ Do they restore your soul? If not, what could you do to give your soul the rest it needs?

Conclusion

Sometimes life—and, admit it, Christianity—seems like such hard work. And it can be. But it isn't meant to be drudgery. Our efforts certainly aren't meant to be endless. We really are supposed to work hard and then play hard!

But, you protest, even our play time is supposed to be spiritual! We can't even have a party without bringing God into it! Well, for one thing, the Bible never says that every get-together has to include hymn singing. Surely God enjoys a good, hearty laugh as much as anyone—why else would He have dressed penguins in tuxedos? Or instilled in so many of us such an irrepressible sense of humor? Or made sure "merry hearts" got into Proverbs? God wants us to have fun. But He also wants us to remember Him . . . because after all, He is the source of all good things. He takes care of us, loves us, wants the best for us. And what could be more restful than remembering that?

Memory Verse

"The Lord is my shepherd, I shall lack nothing. He makes me lie down in green pastures, he leads me beside quiet waters, he restores my soul" (Ps. 23:1-3a).

---

1 *Webster's Ninth New Collegiate Dictionary* (Springfield, Mass.: Merriam-Webster Inc., 1986).

EIGHT

Holiness in Temptation

*H*oliness in temptation? Sounds like a contradiction in terms. But being tempted is not, in itself, sin. It's how we respond to temptation that makes the difference. Today's lesson shows us how to respond to temptation in a holy manner.

Reflection Questions

What are the most common types of temptation you face?

How do you usually handle them?

Introduction

Temptation isn't sin. Even Jesus was tempted to sin! And so was every other Bible character. Their stories give us some practical strategies for turning away temptation when it comes our way. Let's read what happened to Eve, Joseph, and Jesus and see what we can learn.

Study

Read Genesis 3:1-13, 39:1-21, and Matthew 4:1-11.

1. What were the characters of these stories tempted with?

2. What lies were involved in the temptations?

3. Joseph and Jesus resisted the temptations thrown their way. What methods did they use?

4. Eve's first sin was eating the fruit from the forbidden tree, but that was the culmination of several mistakes. What was the progression of events that led to eating the fruit?

⤚ Explain what she could have done differently at each juncture that could have made a difference in the outcome.

5. Giving in to temptation rarely ends with only one sin. List the sins that resulted from the eating of the fruit.

Now read Psalm 119:11; Matthew 6:9-13, 26:41; 1 Corinthians 10:13; 2 Corinthians 11:14; Ephesians 6:11-18; 2 Timothy 2:22-26; James 4:7; 1 Peter 5:8-9.

1. How is Satan described in these passages?

⤚ What do these descriptions tell you about him?

2. From these passages and the stories you read earlier, what do you think Satan's chief strategies are in getting you to sin?

3. Why do you think he is so interested in getting you to sin?

4. Eve didn't see temptation coming. Where did the temptation really begin, and why do you think Satan started that way instead of just dangling the fruit in front of her? How does this fit with the descriptions of him in the New Testament passages?

5. From these passages and the stories you read earlier, what are some strategies you can use to resist temptation?

Application

1. Since we can be assured of receiving forgiveness (1 John 1:9), why should we be so concerned with avoiding temptation?

⌒ Be honest now . . . hasn't the thought of guaranteed forgiveness ever entered your mind when temptation is reeling you in? If so, where do you think that thought comes from?

2. Go back to the temptations you listed in the Reflection Questions. Which of the strategies discussed today would be most helpful in fighting them?

3. Satan is a known liar, but he is very good at making his lies sound like truth. He's able to make those lies sound like our own voice inside our head, and he can make them come out through other people's mouths. He also knows which lies are most effective with each person. Which lies does he frequently use on you, and whose voice does he speak in?

4. What situations do you know to avoid, simply because you can't resist the temptations you find there?

5. Sometimes it seems that certain temptations are all but impossible to overcome. But that, too, is a lie. In what can you take hope and strength?

Conclusion

Satan is a schemer and a liar, and he wants nothing more than to trip you up and lure you away from God. Put that together with our basic sin nature and you've got trouble! But "the one who is in you is greater than the one who is in the world" (1 John 4:4). To be holy in the face of temptation, we just need to listen to the right voice.

Memory Verse

"No temptation has seized you except what is common to man. And God is faithful; he will not let you be tempted beyond what you can bear. But when you are tempted, he will also provide a way out so that you can stand up under it" (1 Cor. 10:13).

NINE

Holiness in Testing

*I*n the last lesson, we learned how to respond to temptation with holiness. Today, we'll study how to respond to testing with holiness. Sometimes they feel very much the same, but they have different sources and purposes.

Reflection Questions

What is the difference between temptation and testing?

How does testing make you feel?

Introduction

We didn't like tests when we were in school, and we don't like them any better in life! Obviously, we dislike them most because they are uncomfortable. But they also show us for who we really are, and that can make us squirm in our seats.

Every Christian has been tested at one time or another, including those in the Bible. The most familiar story of testing, of course, is found in the Book of Job. Let's look at part of Job's story today, along with several other passages of Scripture, and find out what testing is, what it is for, and how to handle it in a holy manner.

Study

Read Job 1:1–2:10; Zechariah 13:9; James 1:2-5, 12; 1 Peter 1:6-7.

1. In the Book of Job, when asked where he had been, Satan said he had been roaming the earth. Why do you think he was doing that?

2. In the conversation between God and Satan, did you notice that it was God who brought up the subject of Job? Why do you think He did so?

3. What do you think Satan hoped to prove by attacking Job's comfortable life?

4. In school, at least part of the reason for testing is so that the teacher can know how the students are progressing. God knows everything; He has no need of a test to let Him know how we are doing. So what do you think the purpose of testing is?

5. Do you think the real benefit of testing lies in the outcome or in the testing process itself, or both? Explain your answer.

➔ What are the benefits of testing?

6. Most people fear tests in school, primarily because they are apprehensive about the results. What do you think happens when we fail God's tests, as we inevitably will at times? (See Lam. 3:22-23; Ps. 117:2; Eph. 2:4-9; James 5:11.)

7. The following passages help us to see some of the things God is looking for when He tests us. What are they?

~ Exodus 16:4

~ Deuteronomy 8:1-5

~ Judges 2:20-22

~ Judges 3:1-4

~ 1 Chronicles 29:17

∽ Psalm 17:3

∽ 1 Corinthians 3:10-15

Application

1. How do you react when you hear the word *testing* in relation to God? Why?

2. Have you ever experienced times of testing? If so, what were they like?

∽ When you look back on those times, how do you feel about them?

➢ Have you been able yet to see the benefits of the testing?

3. Do you suspect that you are in a time of testing right now? What "subject" do you think you are being tested in?

4. What do you think the differences are between *testing* and *temptation?*

➢ Are there temptations to be found within times of testing?

➢ If you currently are being tested, what temptations do you face?

5. Even if you are not being tested currently, you will be eventually; every Christian will be. What can you do to prepare for the test:

～ so that you will pass it?

～ so that you can endure it?

6. We read earlier about God's mercy. How can you reconcile God's mercy with the testing that He allows—and sometimes engineers?

Conclusion

The story of Job is almost too painful to read. For most of us, we have a hard time seeing God giving His permission for such suffering to be inflicted on anyone, let alone such an undeserving person as Job. Yet it's His very mercy that drives Him to do it. He loves us—way too much to let us flounder around in ignorance of who we really are and who He really is. It's in times of testing that we are reduced to bare-bones reality. There's no sugarcoating of our faith or maturity or steadfastness . . . and there's no disguising the sovereignty of our Lord. Sometimes the tests are minor ones. Sometimes they feel like midterm exams. Sometimes they prick us like an itchy clothing tag on our neck; sometimes they devastate us. Sometimes they're designed to make us look at ourselves; always, they're designed to help us see God.

When testing comes, don't resist it. And don't resist God's comfort in the midst of it. He loves you . . . and that's really all you need to know.

Memory Verse

"Consider it pure joy, my brothers, whenever you face trials of many kinds, because you know that the testing of your faith develops perseverance. Perseverance must finish its work so that you may be mature and complete, not lacking anything" (James 1:2-4).

TEN

Leaving a Holy Legacy

lmost every family has its traditions. Turkey at Thanksgiving, ham on Easter . . . presents Christmas morning or presents Christmas Eve . . . nine-layer dip on Superbowl Sunday. In and of themselves, these rituals aren't important, but they mean something to us all the same. They give us foundations, the assurance that some things in our changing lives stay the same. They make us feel connected to each other through shared experiences and memories. But they can be even more than that. Read on to find out how your family memories can be holy ones.

Reflection Questions

What traditions does your family have?

How did those traditions get started?

Introduction

If there was ever a culture that loved traditions, it's the Jewish people. Their calendar makes the Christian calendar look downright boring! It's full of festivals and holy days, and all of them have historical significance, commemorating God's faithfulness to His people. In Old Testament days, there were, of course, no photo albums or video cameras. So today we are going to look at some events in Joshua's story and see the way he found of marking the memories of his people so that they would not be forgotten.

Study

Read Joshua 4:19-24; 7:19–8:2, 28-30; 10:16-27; 22:26-29; 24:22-27.

1. What events prompted the making of the stone monuments?

➣ Why do you think it was important to mark and remember these particular events?

2. In our country, we have a number of monuments to help us remember things that are of national importance. Do you think our monuments are similar in nature to those of the Jewish people? What are the similarities and what are the differences?

3. What was the primary purpose of the monuments of Israel?

4. Joshua 24:29 tells us that Joshua died after erecting the final monument. Why do you think he wanted the last stone to be positioned near "the holy place of the Lord" (v. 26; see also Gen. 12:6-8)?

Application

1. The stone monuments that Joshua built were his legacy to his people. As long as the stones were in place, they would remember the central focus of his life—and be pointed in that direction themselves. Think about the significant people in your childhood. What was important to them? What did they build monuments to in your mind?

⤺ What things will your children remember as being important to you?

＞ What would you like them to remember as being important to you?

2. It doesn't always take a big event to point to what's important in your life. Sometimes, it's just the small choices we make every day that tell our children what we value. Are there any choices you make consistently that might be giving your children a message you don't want them to receive? If so, what are they?

＞ What small things could you do each day to help them be assured of the positive things that you value?

3. It's also good to have some more elaborate traditions that help form a family identity. You likely already have several, but have you evaluated them to see whether they really achieve the purpose you intend for them? Discuss the way you celebrate the following events (or choose some others that are more pertinent to your family). Write the things you generally do on these occasions; what you intend for the events to accomplish; and whether or not you think they really do accomplish these things. If they do not, brainstorm some ideas that might be more effective.

～ Christmas

～ Easter

～ Thanksgiving

～ Fourth of July

～ Family Birthdays

4. God is at work in our families all the time, guiding us, protecting us, providing for us . . . but sometimes we get so caught up in daily life that we forget to notice. What could you do to draw attention to the little things He does for us every day?

➲ How could you commemorate the times when you've seen His hand in a bigger way, such as providing a job after a layoff or keeping you safe in an accident?

➲ Take some time to recall those memorable acts of God in your life.

Memory Verse
"Look to the Lord and his strength; seek his face always. Remember the wonders he has done, his miracles, and the judgments he pronounced"
(1 Chron. 16:11-12).